T0286515

ᏰᏁᏆ

OSKANA POETRY & POETICS

M.W. Jaeggle

Wrack Line

University of Regina Press

Printed and bound in Canada at Imprimerie Gauvin. The text of this book is printed on 100% post-consumer recycled paper with earth-friendly vegetable-based inks.

Cover art: "Northern Acorn Barnacles (Semibalanus balanoides)" by Ryan Hodnett/CC-BY-SA-4.0

Cover and text design: Duncan Campbell, University of Regina Press

Series Editor: Randy Lundy
Managing Editors: Kelly Laycock
    and Shannon Parr
Proofreader: Donna Grant

The text and titling faces are Arno, designed by Robert Slimbach.

Library and Archives Canada Cataloguing in Publication

Title: Wrack line / M.W. Jaeggle.

Names: Jaeggle, M. W., author.

Series: Oskana poetry & poetics.

Description: Series statement: Oskana poetry & poetics | Poems. | Includes index.

Identifiers: Canadiana (print) 20230227449 | Canadiana (ebook) 20230227481 | ISBN 9780889779532 (softcover) | ISBN 9780889779556 (EPUB) | ISBN 9780889779549 (PDF)

Classification: LCC PS8619.A34 W73 2021 | DDC C811/.6—dc23

10 9 8 7 6 5 4 3 2 1

UNIVERSITY OF REGINA PRESS
University of Regina
Regina, Saskatchewan
Canada S4S 0A2
TELEPHONE: (306) 585-4758
FAX: (306) 585-4699
WEB: www.uofrpress.ca
EMAIL: uofrpress@uregina.ca

We acknowledge the support of the Canada Council for the Arts for our publishing program. We acknowledge the financial support of the Government of Canada. / Nous reconnaissons l'appui financier du gouvernement du Canada. This publication was made possible with support from Creative Saskatchewan's Book Publishing Production Grant Program.

for Aubrey

CONTENTS

One

Two

Three

Four

ONE

AUTUMN, ACCORDING TO CHILDHOOD

I.

Your mother whispers your name, draws your eyes away from the
loon threading water, tight stitch. Look, she says. Look: there's a deer
chewing dandelion, right here in the yard. Knees bending, she slowly
breaks distance. But you don't move, you just look. Fuzzy two-point
scraping the ground. Yellow hanging from charcoal, leathery lip. The
arch of its back as it saunters closer. Your mother feeds it, with restless
grace. She's feeding the buck in a long olive dress. She's feeding the
buck a copse of dandelion. Then there's saying goodbye, because it's
time to sit through school with nothing on your mind but the deer.

II.

Hacksaws, rusted blades, hammers, wrenches, measuring tape—a
cornucopia of utility sprawled on the garage table. And beneath a
wall-mounted clock, *Manure Happens.* Your father bracing the thing
as it swings from the ceiling. Pass him the other knife. No, not that
one, the bigger one. Spotted the buck from the kitchen window, he
says. Canyoubelieveit? Sowhatdoyouthink? You think the entrails
slumping over its head look like a cow's out-turned tongue. There's
green stocks jutting through torn intestine and there's yellow dandelion
florets along the pink skin like scales and there's feeding the buck,
saying goodbye, getting into the car, school, then saying goodbye.

SING AGAINST THE LAKE

after Denise Levertov

There it was, confronting him—a lake and the retreating light.
Before night came down, before the darkness could take him,
it struck his side. The blow rang out within his frame,
rather than softened—or perhaps, when it hit him
what he heard was his voice projecting across the water,
the oar cutting through the thought,
his mind treading possibility: watery pitch,
cries swallowed, cold joints, a muted heart.

In the morning, he heard the chorus of the loons,
saw their notes split fog and uncover the cascara near the shore.
Those sensitive to circumstance hold against the blow,
he said as he brought the teacup to his lips,
then they find an inner pew and sing.

UBI SUNT

Not closer to the words petrified by use
but closer to the wind's dry flowing

and the gossip exchanged between aster
and the lance-tip leaves exiled from the Salal bush.

Appetite without measure or shadow, the ground
in August this far from the Fraser

desires only the shadow of clouds. Snow nears though—
you can hear it. You can hear it laugh

where the clay cracks its lip on the bone-edge
of the trail. What was the shrill

of insipid grass just then
but the patient soil whispering in its ear,

repeat a word enough
and it'll turn into water.

CHETAMON MOUNTAIN, JASPER

To the boy
whose mother kneeled before him
and said, at first gently, then curt and glib

    I know you want to stay
    but do you
            understand
    we have to go now
    we just gotta get back on the road
    are you even listening to me
    listen
    you can see the mountain from the car

    look at what you've done
    you've gone and ruined your shirt
    the one grandma got for you

    it's soaking wet
    from your crying
    now let's stop all this and go

    there's juice and chips in the car.

To the boy
who couldn't part from the sight
of the pines enclosing
the rib-like slopes   the crags
checkered with late-day sun
how do I tell you
that you are old enough
that you will remember this spot

north of Jasper   east of the Athabasca
where time was little more than the distance
between a hawk's sharp clear scream
and the roar of a passing semi?

SNOWY OWL

It quits the fog,
effortlessly folds intention,
like newspaper underneath kindling,

then, relinquishing hesitation,
slings itself forward,
flaring against the thick air
like a match along a strike box.

Each stage of itself softly burning away,
taking up the field at present,
swoops, then

        makes its liking
        in the still wake
        of itself.

≈

A hungry snowy owl, a generous window,
tawny switchgrass in the morning light—the given,

letting me silently apprentice
on the refuge that is solitude,

when the closest thing to another human form
is the corner post of a fence.

BECOMING THE GROUND

Beneath a Pacific silver fir, its canopy,
I feel the sword fern,
feel its serrated edges fuse to my calf.

Seagulls rise over Howe Sound,
fold into mercury sky, the kiln air columns.

The Chief sheers, levels the Sea to Sky,
peak to peak,
the trees, doughy, fall inward and resign.

Granite made to kneel on the colony,
prostrate before the sky.

As the word is stripped from the flesh,
scattered by the wind,
and touches everything and nothing
like sex between strangers,

bark, fjord, speaking, cocoon, lips, language, twig

are made to taste the same,
are wrought catholic to the touch.
Then description ceases.

The tree presses, bark scours my back.
Pacific silver fir, *Abies amabilis*.

Here, *I* is no history. Now,
I am time, tree litter, a lovely
silver resin, stratum from the side,
palimpsest from above.

Like relief tapping attentiveness on its shoulder,
I slept when I imitated the memory
of a sleeper's breathing.

But I don't convince myself anymore.
This willed effort is as pointless
as imagining my adulthood spent

in the fort we made as kids, flanked everywhere
by the bramble we called Death Valley,
its thorns piercing the hairless legs under our jeans.

The fort was near the four-cylinder
we dug up with our hands and declared a site
of great archeological importance—so great

it had to be kept a secret, so great we spat
then shook on it, just as our parents
called us home as it got dark.

Here I am in the culvert where we found a car's side mirror.
Here I am in the field of horsetails,
in the blackberry with stained fingers.

Here, there's no wristwatch on a nightstand,
just a mind kidding around
someplace unaware it's unawake.

If I look up at the canopy now, the day's
a shredded rag. If I close my eyes,
the light is honeycombed.

Amid all this tall green life
it's not the mimicry of sleep that brings it about,
but the work of imagining what it is to dream

at the edge of attention's parapet.

LETTER TO A FRIEND
CONCERNING ANOTHER'S WHEREABOUTS

He's at that cabin on the Cariboo plateau,
that one he's always yapping about,
washing chipped bowls with lake water,
careful not to get needle-thin bones stuck in the drain.
He keeps the big red gate locked, the chintz curtains closed.
The garden, long gone to thistle, is home
to his eggshells, burnt barley, soup dregs.
Nothing to stop him from mundane pleasures,
catching rainbow trout only to release them,
noon-warm tea with Kundera, a few laughs
from Diefenbaker on vinyl.
He's in the cabin at the end of Antoine Lake Road,
counting cracks in the foundation, where the rooms
are parting ways. He's in that tin-roof tinderbox,
cataloguing birds, flowers, stones,
watching Bogart movies,
reconciling Clapton with Buddhism.
If you were to ask him if it gets lonely
in the hush of the cabin, he'd say
he's distracted easily.

WATER PUMP VERNACULAR

The pump has been broken
a few days now,
the gasket's on back order,
but no worries,
you'll do just fine hauling water.
There'll be water enough to boil the greens.

In the shed, you'll find
one of them white five-gallon buckets,
head down to the dock,
half of the dock is in the mud, lake's so low,
so be careful,
put the bucket in too fast
and you'll pull up
mud, leaves, and leeches.

Bend your knees,
tilt the bucket
so its level with the surface,
then drop it into the water gently,
being sure
to shift your weight as you make an arc,
letting the weight of the water
draw the bucket in deeper.

If you do it right
your water will come up the colour
of weak green tea.

And if you did the job quietly,
when you turn back toward the cottage,
you might be lucky,
you might be able to name

whatever small, quick animal it is
that has parted the grass
and dug a hole
at the foot
of where a beaver made quick work of a tree.

SPRUCE AND POLLEN

A dozen robins rise from the salmonberry patch,
        ochre before a timid sun.

The spruce, its mess of knots, grooves, signets of life,
speaks from beneath the earth marked with dandelion seeds.

The spruce tells me I am the wind
between thistle needles, that you are the waves
joining Haida Gwaii and the mainland;
        it tells me that the runoff from your palms
        is a salve for distance.

I heed the spruce, tuck the dandelion seeds into my hand.

Here is the virtue that grants symmetry
to a handful of flowers,
what seals our hands when we cup water
for another's lips.

Be in me as still as the cold harbour
       under the morning skies, and not

as the jib unfurled on the deck,
       wet thing under the ochre lamp.

Be in me as the collar against the chin,
       the sleeve loose against the wrist.

See in these hands experience, a winter-cracked
       pity for all that is indefinitely housed.

Baton against my cage or shoreline stray—
       continue as you will, as you are.

KUNDALINI STRAND

I found two strands of your hair on me today.
Reading, I let you fall
upon my shirt. You curled
on my chest
like a snake, the soft rattle
in the sand, the sage.

≈

If I liken these strands
to the crescent flight of the deer,
the plumage of the goldfinch,
reedgrass in autumn light, all this

it's so that when you run toward me
I bend in the river sedge—this time, though,
prepared for your elevation,
the coiled snake at the base of my spine.

A SMALL POEM

as crucial as the space
between prayer beads,

one yellow yarn blouse button.

POEM IN THE MANNER OF WANG WEI

Each time on a well-marked and auspicious day, waiting,
a metic again in some new place,

the thought of you outside the terminal sharpens,
a narrow band of silver on a lake come midnight,

then, far away, there at the baggage carousel,
hawthorn beside fir and cottonwood, you short person you.

INHIBITION

Beyond the lighthouse beams,
there's only the sound of water:
coves exhaling wave, receding,
the thickness of being.

Call to the earth and sea half-held by the night.
It doesn't matter
who sounds out and who listens,
only that someone's near.

You hear the lulls of sand enveloped
by the slow serrated edge of the sea.

If, just like the meeting of the waves
and the land, you return,
what does your presence say about nakedness?

If you undress in the dark, or don't,
will you wake up in any way changed?

PARALLAX

Where does not matter,
though, it must be a place

where your heels remain
poised, a slow breath

across the wheat prairie,
where your legs lunge

forward, a cedar branch
grazing the river's surface,

where your thought strikes the match,
your voice ends the flame,

where you underwrite the word,
become the force behind

golden grassland, temperate rainforest,
a campfire after rain.

THE QUAY

The grey wingtips of seagulls latch onto air,
catch patron winds,

stitched and tended crab traps drop over
the dock, lines slip through

bait-lathered hands, other traps are thrown
sunwards into the ocean

and I wonder if these rhythmic movements are
acrobatic, aerobatic,

if the timbre of the gulls, the grumbling crabbers
were designed to complement

the boulevard planks
or the arid breeze.

If this set was torn down, the wind dismantled,
the waterfront folded into the earth's suitcase,

would the sea, the sea,
motion still, then repeat?

No more calls, no more reading,
and no more scrolling, for there is nothing new to see,
and let there be no more speaking for a while, please.
There is nothing left to do tonight,
no little dilemma, conundrum,
ploy to suffer through.
Yesterday, I was on the edge of it,
that sense in which the body's rhythms
dictate the clock's plodding,
when we unknowingly retreat into repose.
But then things happened, an interruption.
Somehow, I fucked up a baked potato.

Now, though, I have found the time,
given myself to it, feel it as it is.
Perhaps circumstance is orbit rather than being:
an interior hurricane, myself the focus,
the still middle of it all.
In the land of voices, pitch, and colour,
sigh methodically at the grace which comes
from being that stillness. Breathe slowly,
not out of helplessness
but out of reserve for the starchy goodness
you will come to know.

Even if you're right and there's a difference
between a body awash with sweat,
a fermenting midden
wending slowly from sleep to hunger,

and a body harangued by a fissile stomach,
a riotous ambivalence, at once a need and disgust
for a thing as simple as an oatcake—I mean,

even if there is a difference, I'd say I'm shapeshifting
from Lurch to greasefiend now, becoming animal
in the wake of last night's picklebacks, shooing you

out of the dark unkept kitchen
so you can't decry this goat
hung over the kitchen sink, bespeckling beard
with toast, runny egg, animal crackers.

ARBUTUS BREATH

It is the arbutus tree's
thin paper bark that

dries in the salt air
curls and falls to the roots

collects with the pulpy fruit
as above the branches turn

into the yellow boas of mythology
which gather to form a story:

the seeds to a Greek epic
sprouting for the seasonal verse

grown on no Aegean coastline
but on the Sea to Sky

misunderstood by the coldest
of cold shoulders

those who expect more from Pacific *fjords*
and sixteen lines on an ectopic tree.

ON BOULEVARD DE L'ACADIE

Walking back to my place
after the Tarkovsky matinée,
we pass an alley and see
an old mattress,
a torn garbage bag,
and a falcon lodge its beak
into a starling, tear
the skin from its neck,
and fly off with a piece
of its syrinx.

I can't make out what you're thinking
as we continue down the street.
There's no expression on your face,
though your reticence
reminds me of the silence that passed over us
twenty minutes ago, back on the Metro.

Compassion toward all beings,
that's what I get from his films.
Above all, compassion toward those that sing.

That's what you said at Jean-Talon station,
before the bells chimed, the doors closed,
and the train started up again.

The teacher walks through the house
written the night before,
locating as best as she can
from the placement of a closet, a sconce,
or the outlets, where the writer,
if he hadn't been so quick
to frame and drywall,
might have included external sources of light.

PARC-EXTENSION, LATE FEBRUARY

I need to get to Hochelaga,
the stranger says from his car's window,
I'm so late for dinner. It's my mother's birthday.
His car is stuck in the snow, the engine pained,
and you, you're mired
in his carbon footprint, pushing with your hands,
then with your ass against the license plate.

In the window of a nearby restaurant, you see
a young girl chewing on naan,
butter chicken on her nose—
she's laughing at you, wiping the foggy window
with her wrist to improve the view.

Hell, why not encourage it?
Laughter's good for digestion
and what's pride during winter when the clouds
retch and everyone, displumed of dignity,
dons layers to shovel
or plant heels and heave and

this time the rustbit Honda rises from its grave,
which means down you go, Dom Pérignon,
christening the dirty bumper with your forehead.

The dutiful son, flirting with a red light
and tapping the horn as thanks, putters away.
Like a matriarch on a Liverpool dock, hanky in hand,
you wave toward the car, for there's a chance
your karma is looking back at you.

You turn toward the girl, a cameo
bordered by condensation,
her forehead now pressed against the glass,
she's laughing and laughing.
Her adult teeth have yet to come in.

WOOL OVERCOAT

A woman in a green plaid dress, bending
cautiously over a wide, shallow bowl.

Her freckled hands wringing her hair like a terry cloth.
Her face turned away from you, toward the window,

where pigeons fly upward with great effort, then fall
as if they were tossed pamphlets.

The door through which you entered creaks,
causing her to turn toward you. Drops of sun-caught quartz

fall from her chin, ding the side of the bowl,
and pool on the floor. You can see now, this woman

is your grandmother as she is in a photograph from 1953.
Barefoot, walking toward a suitcase opened on a wicker chair,

she tells you that you need to take care of yourself,
that you are tall yet too thin. But you can only say,

I found your wool overcoat in the back of the closet.
In the pocket I found a torn movie ticket,

and by this I remembered you. To which she replies,
while blotting her hair with a shirt,

Well, where is it? Did you bring it with you?
It gets so cold when I walk home from work at night.

ELEGY FOR APRIL

Snowflakes tumbling
from Côte-des-Neiges sky
struggle for clarity
for a sense of what they are
against the falling that obscures them

just as what little I knew of her
what little I remember of her
pains
like the border of an orchard
wishing for the wilderness beyond what it is.

SEHNSUCHT

for Wilhem Karl Jäggle, my great-grandfather

The Karl I know is

   a chainless monocle fixed
   to a worn leather pouch bearing
   Deutschland in small yellow print;
   a bent envelope containing
   one foldable map of Switzerland;
   and one photograph of him
   in 1920-something at a train station
   beneath Timmins train sign,
   contrapposto, all *gravitas*,
   one hand pulling back his pinstripe jacket,
   reaching into pocket for matches,
   the other deftly balancing a cigarette
   and thumbing a flashy tie,
   all centred by a wide-brim Stetson
   tilting darkness across

an unmet face I have inherited
and a handful of warmth.

CANDLES

for Phyllis Webb

I'm learning that there's a difference between the limit
of desire and desire exhausting itself,

that one can wait long enough for the warmth
found in the reticence of a garden,

that it's okay to be as gentle as peach fuzz,
bamboo yarn, a secret,

that privacy itself can be a bright
lodestone,

that separation is a bruise taking the time
to feel and forgive its shape,

that there is a cadence to failure
that unfolds a brilliant shade of blue.

≈

Patience is an answer found in grief:
a knowing that evades intention,
that fickle second skeleton.

What is left of me tries to take after you.
I breathe in the space between the moth and the candle,
where the warmth of the other
tenders the dust of the flame.

≈

I'm not floating across Fulford Harbour
avoiding the wake of the ferry,

nor am I watching the cobalt water turn dove grey.
I'm not the soft fist felt weekly on the radio.

I'm the purple starfish offset with yellow,
that lily you didn't make the subject of a painting.

Somewhere in the life of peacock blue,
so much of what I am

places my ear against a candlelit page,
listening to your footfalls.

≈

And
there
and there and
there
and over   and
over   your mouth

even in silence
continues to sing.

SALMON RUN, HORSEFLY RIVER

On a hot day in early September, standing
knee-deep in the river to cool off, something slick
like a loaded sable brush and the width
of a scarf firmly strikes your calf.

In the water a few feet upstream, the back fin
of a bright-red sockeye sways
like a candle's flame in a drafty room. Its strike
is as close as you will ever get to theophany.

A bald eagle alights on a spruce tree, leans
back and spreads its wings, steadying,
steadying its outpost. Crimson flesh
courses through the water, but it does not move.

Five more red backs dart through
the platinum-glint riffle, where the water's surface
is knuckled with granite stones, but again,
the eagle does not descend.

In the shadow of a nurse log on which you sit
and tie your laces, a wood frog
balances between its eyes a waterdrop, a node
from Indra's net.

In the middle of the path that will take you home,
inert like a garden figurine, a robin
holds a writhing worm in its beak. What's attentiveness
if it's not a basket with which to gather things?

You catch yourself motionless, too,
listening to the salmon swim against the current,
an old song made of water, rock,
muscle, and bone.

Ask me whether what I have done is my life,
and I will say look,
a dowitcher with the head of Janus, one face
revering the wrack line, thumbing with its long bill
what the water has heaved—blanched Pepsi caps,
mummified kelp, sticks sea-eaten and stripped clean.

Ask me whether what I have done is my life,
and whether it has made a difference,
and I will reply—but only to admit that,
like anything committed to the sea,
maybe I'll get back to you in the morning.

Notice the other half, the face fixed to the sky,
it hears only the bill nicking shells, tapping lure.
He wants to have a name ready
for the music that will appear when bottle glass,
once shard but now a rounded green, is juggled
between their clicking chopstick beaks.

Ask me whether what I have done is enough,
and I will say let there be the loss that a wrack line records,
if only for how the cold air whistles on a beach,
while we suture
our broken and partial worlds
with seagrass left behind by the tide,
each in our own way a historian of waves.

TWO

there was the ticking
of sleet on frozen snow
while your brother
came down the front steps
hauling his gear.

I gripped the steering wheel,
teetered between the state I was in
after five or six
and the thought of telling him
No, I can't drive you like I said I would
because I've been drinking in the basement.

We were late for practice
and there was that icy bridge
signalled by the hill,
the one which would lift you a little
off your seat, reminding you
there's always the company of gravity.

And there was time slackening
when I lost control on the ice,
his hockey sticks grating
the ribbed back of the truck
sounding in the darkness
like cans
crunched by a fist
in a windowless room.

I remember the truck wrapped around
a Sitka spruce, the headlights
reaching into the darkness
as if it could be dug out like marrow,
the wiper blades screeching over cracked glass,
a single tire spinning its last life,
a branch in his throat, a clear taste to the air
as I ran down the road and yelled,
and the question of cause—
me or the land.

They found me passed out under a telephone pole
at the foot of someone's long driveway.
They said there had been an accident,
that I had a broken arm,
that my wife and daughter were on their way,
but I kept saying,
My son is twelve years old,
I need to get him to a hockey game
in Prince George.

And I remember, a few months after you had left
with your mother, driving past
Vancouver's sour canneries,
chicken-rendering plants, and the last
pulp mill, cold air crept
along my forearm just outside Hope.

There, I tasted the same clear air as before
and the meaning of a memory clicked—
how your mother had placed
my empties
on the kitchen table beside a newspaper
open on Noah's obituary.

A THEORY OF WINTER

The wind is always the same in winter;
it always demands an explanation.

Since the work of alcohol outpaces
any chance of understanding,

you, my daughter, have rightfully lived
the past months away in some concrete wilderness,

outgrowing the clothes that I remember you in and the excuse
that you were too young to know what really happened.

When the sun is a rumour, much like today,
this being cloistered inside a winter coat

values little but the telos of breathing,
of *yawning* the world back from the night.

There will be no revolution in me when the weather
changes, when the wind ceases to carry feeling.

The morning after you and your mother left
I washed your dishes for the last time,

keeping my grief at bay by thinking of impossibilities—
where it is that the snow likes to summer,

what sort of blessing might be found in tree litter,
what it'd be like to sand down my shoulders with leaves,

what it would mean to be a white oak tree in March,
my leafless frame scenting the cold air,

and what form my weeping would take if my son,
now a black-capped warbler, branched upon me.

A GAME BETWEEN SIBLINGS

You and your brother made me tip the table on its side.
The enemy is everywhere, Noah had said,
and there's a need for sandbags.
You laughed as you loaded an elastic band, taut
between your finger and thumb.
My cans were lined up on the coffee table,
but you had emptied yourself
of sweetness and light, eager to play your way
until someone's spirit buckled.
You smoked him good above the eye
as he realigned the targets.
You apologized again and again
as if your voice alone could quiet his crying.
When you later told me the table was a bomb shelter,
that it had to return quickly to its upright position,
I was thankful to be of service, taking it to mean
an end to friendly fire.
When I saw your hands over his ears and his hands over yours,
I knew you were both envisioning
sirens and planes overhead.

But this image gives way
to my own sort of play, an imagined reunion.
Your brother backpacking through Europe,
making a visit to the English town you called home,
the lanterns along your street punctuating the night
like laughter notching edges into silence.

The horizon was a thread
between the sea, a faded porcelain blue,
and the sparse grey clouds that left me

sullen yet hopeful, as I was
when I rescued a sparrow from the cat, then
left it breathing in the fork of a tree.

Noah dug up a long band of kelp that day
then snuck up on you. Just as his name
left my lips, the kelp

disintegrated in the arc before the blow.
Disperse, the shore might have said
if it could speak, *disperse*

just as a band of horses might scatter
to avoid an oak
in a sun-drenched grove.

Your wet brown hair was slick like a seal,
Noah kneeled by the water pouting,
and your mother sat beside me on a log, her face upturned,

taking in what was left of the sun.
What are you thinking of?
she asked after a long silence.

Nothing, I replied, *nothing but the right to annoy,*
the birthright of a younger sibling,
and the kelp's hunger for flight.

FORGETTING

What I can remember now
bores me, disgusts me, embarrasses me.

Painting a neighbourless fence.
Dog shit on a summer day.

Tomato sauce on the last white shirt.
Just one more drink.

Forgetting is knowing that the apple tree in the garden
is the upsurge of a lucky pit.

Forgetting is not knowing whether it was the optimism
of my youngest or oldest that parted the soil and dropped the seed.

On the shores of Burrard Inlet, was it you
who upturned the barnacled rocks

and said to each scurrying penny crab,
And where are you off to in such a hurry, Mister?

Was it your brother at the top of the stairs
when I put my wedding ring

on top of the fridge then hissed
at your mother bent over the kitchen sink?

Let me tell you
a moment dissolving into nothingness

is turning your back on a close history,
like building an extension

to a home torn open by a plow wind.

I pick green beans and pull
carrots from the ground, cart them
inside to the kitchen sink.
Leftover venison stew
spreads across a blue speckled plate
and butts up against the vegetables.
I wait for my final coffee to cool.
Eating alone at the hazy window,
I notice a draft gently sway
three stems of sage twist-tied to a nail
above your brother's bedroom door.

Each morning, I walk past that door
and enter the bathroom.
In its small round mirror, I notice my stubble
turning alder and my cheeks
turning into a bruised apricot
from a Flemish painting.

Tonight, though, before entering
the room where I chart my age,
I stand beneath that dry grey sage
and think of entering his room.
But I leave that threshold undisturbed.
The motes of dust
that would rise to meet my presence
would be testimony to what I have done.

I remember opening the closet
to retrieve our coats, a moth the shape
and colour of an old joint embedded
in the armpit of my flannel coat
and you beside me on the floor, declaring
that you were angry because
you no longer liked your shoes, the laces
too light a shade of blue.
I remember another moth, a big one
with yellow owl eyes on its wings, the eyes
staring at me from the bottom
of your glossy pink backpack while it nibbled
on baby carrots turned to mush, a forgotten lunch.
And I remember the drawing of the moth
you pinned to the fridge, and you
tugging on my pant leg, saying,
Dad, did you know that moths evolved
when there were only three types of light?
The sun and the moon and the stars.

As I watch the sun bend over
as if to draw from a well, I realize
that all I am now is what I have seen.
Like the moths gently thudding the porch light,
I replay memories of you and Noah
as if encircling that light
could scour guilt from a body.

THREE

When the stream in the woods runs clear,
the rose blooms, and the nightingale
refines its song as if its throat was whetstone,

like a stream, I should also make myself clear
and whittle the male voice small, a needlepoint beak.

Love from afar, if there is the fear
that separation
leads to amnesia, say
such a complication is a fen.

Let's ford it,
let's ford the distance between staccato, meet

at the flower that is a river mouth,
the estuary where echoes converge,
where you give
what I could never provide for myself:

an antidote to the lyre,
a view of myself from outside,
a view that lets you, O loved being, be.

When persuasion emerged from desire's rib
to bundle the first bouquet,
troubadour
was the name given to the sound
of the bow
tightening.

If I stake myself in the shadow
that marks otherwise,

if I tarry, it's not to learn new knots,
nor to learn new arrangements.

It's only away from the bandstand,
out of the heat,

that I can tutor myself in sincerity,
that I can learn to be more of what I am to you.

≈

A troubadour on the road outside of town, recalling
a glowing account of a princess from Tripoli,

realized his world was at once foreign
and known to him. That was the feeling of standing on

a frozen river with water running underneath,
a layer of certainty overtop a fluid core.

The way women tucked flowers into their hair,
he insisted, were messages meant solely for him,

but in a language he didn't understand.
There's the confidence of this song and dance man,

who later took the cross and put to sea, unaware his fever
was one of his own making. But what I want

is the confidence of the woman who,
while walking toward her work in the vineyard, tucked

a strand of lavender into her hair
for no other reason than the tickle it made against her ear.

I want the certainty of the woman who thought
the road coloured by sunlight swaying through branches

would resemble the brown and black chest of a pheasant
if only that bard, dumbfounded in the middle of it,

would get the hell out of the way.

There are teachers of all persuasions
perched in shore pine,
declaring what they do not deserve
and thereby hope to receive.

But my throat is dried by all this chirping,
by the words cast outward,
outward as if they bring you
to the other shore
rather than line your lungs, outward
as if singing was a skeleton key
clasped to your neck, and not the mortar
you unknowingly apply
to the holes within you
where natural light breaks in.

Love from afar, if I speak plainly,
not as a bray, a crusader,
but in the vernacular of seed, petal,
moss skein by the stream,
be that spectre with legs crossed, smiling
on the fading edge of a recurring dream.

We'll call this morning ritual,
the way sunlight hits
where you will sleep upon your return,
a reminder that so much of what we call life
is waiting.

What some call nourishment
is left at the door
of my mind in a leaflined basket
by a nightingale loving love.

What am I to myself
that must be insisted upon so often?
Is it that knowing the difference between
recalling and projecting love
is distancing the poverty of a fantasy
from the freedom of parallel lines?

      A silhouette collapsing distance
      will never be as brilliant, then,

      as you in that neon orange jacket
      taking your boots to the rain beside me.

Not the crusader caped and staffed,
nor a hunched bird's back.

No to the gifts of May, too,
parted pink fireweed.

There, down the game trail,
no, not the meaning of rocks
accustomed to moss,
whatever that may be.

There, fixed to an exposed root
a stone's throw from the creek,
there,
       all hortative, all clutched being,
       all *pick me, O pick me,*
a model
for this form of solitude:

the dandelion
dreaming its domicile,
dreaming itself yellow and green.

≈

That we once saw a moonset.
That we sat
on granite outcrop,
hands in root-nerved soil.
That we heard
the responsibility of crickets.
That there was a density to things
but no weight.
That there is
no need to imagine otherwise.

～

Down with pledges and pleas,
love collaborates,
love consorts with friendship
to become a nest, a dwelling.

So when the nightingale in the woods
joyously beholds its own making,
and the stream is clear,
and the wind in season
sings through the grain,

it's no statement,
no male boldness belying honest love,
that follows

but modestly preening words,
slowly bending emphasis into rising intonation,
the openness of a lilt,

are you truly hidden
if I see you in everything?

FOUR

COLVILLE'S HORSES

You return to the field mice rushing between tufts of grass,
the unpainted birds really there only in mind,
the red horse with each heavy step shedding its colour
to the well-worn path cutting through the pasture.

Everything is as the cloud—fluent in leaving.
But what about when the wind extracts tears from your eyes?
Any traces of those who were exiled are overgrown and buried,
time-tinted, like an afterthought of pink flowers.

What you're feeling is an abbreviation for a word you don't know.
How does the present tense pivot in history?
It's how a cross in a field can be Janus-faced,
at once a memorial and a celebration of expulsion.

It's such a question, you think, pulling a string fixed to a woman's shoulder,
compelling her head to turn back, as if somebody had called out her name.

French Cross, 1988.

Compelling her head to turn back, as if somebody had called out her name,
is that other species of thought—a memory, this one of a sister's death.

A woman in a yellow dress descending from a horse is taken
by a memory and the idea that everything cherished
plays too close to a shoreline after heavy rain, then cascades,
like leaves through dense branches, into the Shubenacadie.

She remembers hearing her sister's cries from the river at daybreak.
She remembers gravity releasing its tethers, becoming the name
for kicking the milk pail over, knocking the barn door off its track,
hitting a fence post at full stride, unearthing a nest of mice.

Barefoot at the edge, *duende* dancing to the heartbeat
against her collar and the sight of her piebald horse out in the field,
steam rising off its back. There she had said to herself,
if I have ever known softness, it's somewhere in that smoke.

Girl on Piebald Horse, 1952

If I have ever known softness, it's somewhere in that smoke,
the deft touch of it crossing the nightfelt field,
matching the islands in the sky like the memories of siblings
or the grain of two violins cut from the same tree.

But this is the work of the Tantramar Marsh, just another way
to note the absence of the sun, the depth of forest green,
how the train stealing the horizon is symbol for colonial thinking,
and how the crossties count down the horse's heartbeats.

If you could ask two rivals for the meaning of horsepower,
would you be satisfied if their replies were both order?
Would this answer sound like guidance, but feel like force?

Like everything held too close for too long, it's forgotten
that you don't see the horse's eyes. But if you did,
how quickly would you shift your sympathy to a train?

Horse and Train, 1954

How quickly would you shift your sympathy to a train?

A past me would have believed there's a right answer
to such a question, taking it as a provocation,
as morning daylight once felt when I opened the curtains.

But now, spoken by a woman on a horse replete with midnight blue,
it's the pencilled outline or first brushstroke—a necessary start.

Admit the powerlines edging a forest resemble a mandala,
that a grey sky fades into salmon scales,
that a bottomless hill is a form fit for thinking.
Look long enough and a centrifugal voice slowly eddies away
like shoreline weeds carried by a shallow current.

When the woman pushes me for an answer, *How quickly?*
I simply carry my eyes across the stream of myself and say,

As slowly as a persimmon sweetens in the sun.

Horse and Girl, 1984

As slowly as a persimmon sweetens in the sun
let me put you in this picture:

under the faintest sliver
of light light blue
in cloud-impasto sky

three arched horse backs
between spokeless wheels
hay bales   a barn   one sooty belfry
sigh
relieved to glimpse blue

no not that dormant detail behind all hearts
there   there in that small stretch of sky

the blue framing the faces in the water trough
as clearly as a sliver nags a nerve.

Three Horses, 1946

As clearly as a sliver nags a nerve,
spots of blue and yellow throb behind the eye.

If you follow the horses circling in your mind long enough
sounds marble into cacophony, like wind
through willow tree, hail on tin roof or back porch.

But eventually, the hooves pounding the gravel in mind
make the sound of *enough*. Eventually, it is enough to know
that faceless men float behind pacing hearts,
that control need not mean the use of reins,
that the inner voice flattens like a wave crest,

and that what comes before that *enough* is simply
a dwelling for hesitation, the mind's feuding roommates.

But when you find yourself again a vessel for worry you might think
this scene is missing something.

Two Pacers, 1951

This scene is missing something:
a weathervane, a curtained window, a nest under the eaves.
But this, too, is another way to note your apprehension,
that the sun, tied to some distant fence post, is whimpering.

You might think there's something missing to this building,
but then you read the dark plaque in the centre and say,
Of course, this is a church. But is that relief?
You know there's nothing beyond that white door.

There's only this weather-beaten fence, this flimsy gate,
and a sound which prefigures the presence of change:
the sound of a wet burlap sack giving way to a drum.

A black horse is running toward you on waterlogged grass,
making you wonder if that thudding is your heart,
and what it is you'll forget to say as you're winded at the gate.

Church and Horse, 1964

"Sing against the Lake" is after Denise Levertov's "Variation on a Theme by Rilke," a poem included in *Breathing the Water* (New York: New Directions, 1987).

"Candles" is for the broadcaster, teacher, and poet Phyllis Webb. An earlier version of this poem was longlisted for the 2018 CBC Poetry Prize.

"*Amor de Lonh*" responds to the *vida* and surviving lyrics of the twelfth-century troubadour Jaufré Rudel. I am especially indebted to the translations in Paul Blackburn's *Proensa: An Anthology of Troubadour Poetry* (Berkeley: University of California Press, 1978) and Rupert T. Pickens's *The Songs of Jaufré Rudel* (Toronto: Pontifical Institute of Mediaeval Studies, 1978).

Many of the paintings by Alex Colville spotlighted in "Colville's Horses" are reproduced in David Burnett's *Colville*, a monograph and exhibition catalogue published by the Art Gallery of Ontario and McClelland & Stewart in 1983.

ACKNOWLEDGEMENTS

Thanks to the editors and staff of the following publications, where many of these poems first appeared, sometimes in different form: *The Antigonish Review, Contemporary Verse 2, The Dalhousie Review, Headlights Anthology, Scrivener Creative Review, Soliloquies Anthology, The Veg, where is the river,* and *Sweet Water: Poems for the Watersheds* (Caitlin Press, 2020).

Some of these poems previously appeared in chapbooks. I extend my gratitude to Karen Schindler at Baseline Press for publishing *Janus on the Pacific*; to David Zieroth at the Alfred Gustav Press for publishing *The Night of the Crash*; and to Caryl Peters and Shane Neilson at Frog Hollow Press for publishing *Choreography for a Falling Blouse.*

For his careful editing and sage advice, many thanks to Randy Lundy.

Thanks to Shannon Parr and Kelly Laycock for overseeing the manuscript through production and to Duncan Campbell for designing the cover art.

I am happily indebted to Aubrey Nash and christian favreau for their critical readings and encouragement. May the conversations continue.

Author proceeds from this book will be donated to the Raven legal defense fund for the Wet'suwet'en First Nation.

Born in Vancouver, British Columbia, M.W. Jaeggle is the author of three chapbooks, *Janus on the Pacific*, *The Night of the Crash*, and *Choreography for a Falling Blouse*. He lives in Buffalo, New York, where he is a PhD student in the Department of English at SUNY Buffalo. *Wrack Line* is his first book of poetry.

Ꭰꮎꮆ

OSKANA POETRY & POETICS
BOOK SERIES

Publishing new and established authors, Oskana Poetry
& Poetics offers both contemporary poetry at its best
and probing discussions of poetry's cultural role.

Randy Lundy—*Series Editor*

Advisory Board

Sherwin Bitsui	Tim Lilburn
Robert Bringhurst	Duane Niatum
Laurie D. Graham	Gary Snyder
Louise Bernice Halfe	Karen Solie